Drive and Str

Devon

Michael Bennie

COUNTRYSIDE BOOKS
NEWBURY BERKSHIRE

First published 2006
© Michael Bennie, 2006

COUNTRYSIDE BOOKS
3 Catherine Road
Newbury, Berkshire

To view our complete range of books,
please visit us at
www.countrysidebooks.co.uk

ISBN 1 85306 968 X
EAN 978 1 85306 968 0

Cover picture showing the view towards Seaton from Beer Head
supplied by Derek Forss

Photographs by the author

Designed by Peter Davies, Nautilus Design
Produced through MRM Associates Ltd., Reading
Typeset by Jean Cussons Typesetting, Diss, Norfolk
Printed by Borcombe Printers, Romsey

Contents

AREA MAP SHOWING LOCATIONS OF THE WALKS

Contents

PUBLISHER'S NOTE

We hope that you obtain considerable enjoyment from this book; great care has been taken in its preparation. Although at the time of publication all routes followed public rights of way or permitted paths, diversion orders can be made and permissions withdrawn.

We cannot, of course, be held responsible for such diversion orders and any inaccuracies in the text which result from these or any other changes to the routes nor any damage which might result from walkers trespassing on private property. We are anxious though that all details covering the walks are kept up to date and would therefore welcome information from readers which would be relevant to future editions.

The simple sketch maps that accompany the walks in this book are based on notes made by the author whilst checking out the routes on the ground. However, for the benefit of a proper map, we do recommend that you purchase the relevant Ordnance Survey sheet covering your walk. The Ordnance Survey maps are widely available, especially through booksellers and local newsagents.

Introduction

Bow Creek

Devon is a county of stunning scenery and picturesque villages tucked away down winding lanes or just off the main tourist routes. It is an area of unexpected vistas and hidden treasures, which are often best approached on foot. For only on foot is one travelling at nature's pace, and therefore able to appreciate the wildlife with which our countryside abounds, and the variety of wild flowers in the fields and hedgerows. Only on foot can one be sure not to miss the sudden appearance of a breathtaking view, a picturesque woodland scene or a site of particular natural or historical interest. And discovering Devon on foot is not difficult; we are fortunate in having some 3,000 miles of public footpaths – and that is without taking into account the open spaces of Dartmoor or the newly opened access areas of Exmoor and the East Devon heaths. So wherever you are, there is bound to be an attractive walk nearby.

In this collection, I have tried to provide a taste of the variety of walking experiences available in my county, although with such an extensive network of paths it can obviously only scratch the surface. There is something for everyone: the routes range from 2 to 5 miles and cover the whole county, from the Exmoor coast to the South Hams. Some offer a bit of a challenge – Devon is after all a rugged, hilly county – but many are easy ambles and all are along clear paths and are well within the capability of a moderately fit person. Sketch maps supplement the route descriptions and for each walk there is an indication of the terrain it covers so that you know what you are letting yourself in for. And if you feel the need for refreshment, there are also brief descriptions of pubs in the vicinity – most are at the start of the walk, but a few are along the route and some a few minutes' drive away. I hope you agree with my choices, but please remember that my assessments are subjective and based on my personal criteria.

Finally, I would like to thank my various walking companions: my wife Katy, my son Jonathan, Simon McCandlish, Keith Walter, and Rod and Jill Latham. They have enlivened many of my excursions with enjoyable company and useful comments.

Michael Bennie

1

Lee Bay, Woody Bay and Caffyns Heanton Wood

The gatehouse at Lee Abbey

The Walk 3¼ miles   **Terrain** Some steep climbs initially
Map OS Explorer OL9 Exmoor (GR 695492)

How to get there

Turn west from the centre of Lynton, following the signs for the Valley of Rocks and Lee Bay. **Parking**: There is a small car park above the bay at the end of the Lee Abbey Estate. Note: there is a small toll for crossing the estate; the combined toll and parking fee is payable at the entrance to the car park.

Drive and Stroll

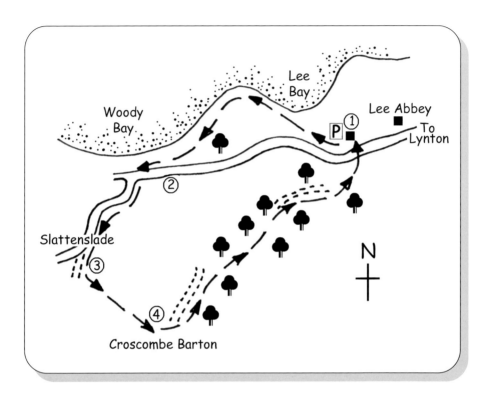

Introduction

Coastal views and woods are the main features of this route. Starting at Lee Bay, part of the Lee Abbey estate, you follow the South West Coast Path round to Woody Bay, with excellent coastal views to keep you company, before heading inland and taking farm paths across to beautiful Regency-built Croscombe Barton. From here you head back to the coast through lovely Caffyns Heanton Wood, with a stream tumbling alongside as you walk. It is a delightfully peaceful walk – even the lanes are almost car-free. Although there are some stiff climbs on the outward stretch the return is easy, and the views along the coast and birdsong in the woods make the effort worthwhile.

The Crown Hotel

Lynton, 1½ miles east of Lee Bay, is home to this attractive 18th century coaching inn. The main bar is a lovely room, divided in two, with an eating area through an arch. It is full of character, with murals on the walls depicting musicians around the fire as well as local scenes. There are welcoming fires in winter, and a covered terrace. It has a reputation for its cask-conditioned ales and its food. The latter ranges from bar snacks and soups to local fish and such tasty meat dishes as Exmoor steak and ale pie. Telephone: 01598 752253.

THE WALK

 (1)

Turn right out of the car park and follow the lane up a hill. It swings right and you get the first of the sea views, across to **Lee Abbey** on the right.

Lee Abbey never was an abbey. It was, in fact, built in about 1850 as a private house, and is now a Christian community, conference centre and holiday complex. Much of the surrounding area is part of its estate. The old gatehouse, which you will have passed on your way to Lee Bay, is particularly fine.

As the lane begins to turn left, branch right, following the **South West Coast Path** sign for **Woody Bay**. It takes you along the edge of the cliff and across a stile. Go down some steps, cross another stile and turn right on the other side to yet another stile, always following the Coast Path signs. Another two stiles follow. The path then swings inland, and half left you will see **Duty Point Tower** on the horizon, guarding **Lee Bay**. Cross another stile and enter a pretty wood filled with rhododendrons. The path climbs

and after a while swings left and finally comes out at the lane.

  (2)

Turn right. The lane continues to climb and after a few hundred yards you come to a junction; go left (signposted to Slattenslade). This lane climbs steeply, and a little under ½ mile beyond the fork, you will come to **Slattenslade**. Just beyond the buildings, turn left along a track (signposted to Croscombe Barton).

 (3)

About 100 yards along the track, you will see a footpath sign pointing left across a stile. Turn off and cross a field to a gate. Keep to the left of the next field to a gate in the far left-hand corner. Continue keeping left as you cross more fields, and you will finally come to a path junction. Turn left across a stile, following the sign for an alternative path avoiding the farmyard. Keep to the right of another field to a gate on the right leading onto a grassy track. Turn right and after a few yards left down some steps, again following the 'alternative footpath' sign. That takes you down a field and across a small footbridge. As you go you will see the impressive buildings of **Croscombe Barton** on your right.

Drive and Stroll

Croscombe Barton was once a priory. It is a magnificent set of buildings dating back to Regency times, and is now holiday accommodation.

Some more steps take you up to a track; turn left, following the bridleway sign.

Follow the track down the valley, with a conifer plantation climbing the slopes on the right and a small stream running alongside you on the left. After 500 yards the track swings sharp left across the stream; go straight on, following the footpath sign for **Lee Abbey** and **Lynton**. Above the stream you will find a clear path.

This is a beautiful woodland stretch. The going is easy, you have the stream cascading over the rocks on your left for company, and the wood is alive with birdsong.

On this spot – 1st April 1780 – nothing happened.

An intriguing sign at Lee Abbey

After about 600 yards or so, climb some steps on the right and join a track; turn left, following the yellow waymark painted on a tree. You then join a clearer track. After a short distance you come to a junction; go straight on (signposted to Lee Abbey, Lynton and Six Acre Cross) and almost immediately left (signposted to Lee Bay). After ¼ mile, go through a gate and cross a lane back to the car park.

Places of Interest Nearby

Just beyond Lynton, about 2½ miles away, is its twin village of Lynmouth, where you will find the **Glen Lyn Gorge**. Telephone: 01598 753207. Also in Lynmouth is the **Exmoor Brass Rubbing Centre**, where you can do your own rubbing. Telephone: 01598 752529.

2 | Hartland Point and Fattacott Cliff

The magnificent view to Hartland Point

The Walk 4¼ or 5½ miles   **Terrain** Just one or two undemanding climbs
Map OS Explorer 126 Clovelly and Hartland (GR 270267)

How to get there

Take the A39 west from Bideford and turn right onto the B3248 for Hartland. Turn right again, following the sign for Hartland Point. From this road, follow the signs for Fattacott and Exmansworthy. **Parking**: In the National Trust car park at Exmansworthy.

Drive and Stroll

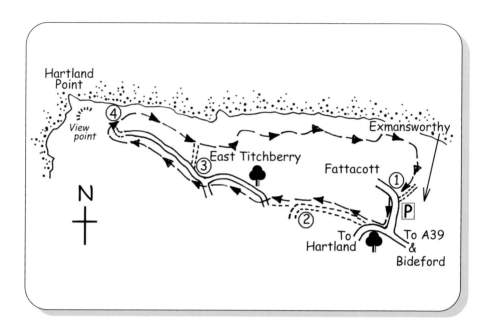

Introduction

Magnificent coastal views combine with pretty, flower-filled hedgerows and farm paths to make this a very special outing. You will follow quiet lanes and tracks, full of natural interest, west to pretty East Titchberry Farm. Here there is a choice: a short cut takes you straight to the South West Coast Path, but you can continue to Hartland Point, with its lighthouse and superb viewpoint. Whichever you choose, the return leg follows the Coast Path, from which you can enjoy more views, both along the cliffs and inland over the green fields.

The Hart Inn

Hartland, 2 miles away, boasts three pubs, all of which have their attractions. My favourite, however, is the Hart, an interesting old hostelry. The entrance leads to a stone passageway, with two snug little rooms on the right and the main bar on the left. At the end is a courtyard, with a door leading to a garden. The bare stone walls and low ceiling give it a lot of character. The food on offer is good traditional pub fare, ranging from baguettes, ploughman's lunches and omelettes to pasties and sausage and chips. Telephone: 01237 441474.

THE WALK

Turn left and follow the lane back for ¼ mile to a T-junction. Turn right (signposted to Hartland and Hartland Point). As you go, there is a pretty view across the fields to your right. After 200 yards pass a small wood on your left and then the lane swings left. As it does so, go straight on along a surfaced track. After a while the futuristic radar dome at **Hartland Point** comes into view, and the rocks of the point itself.

After ½ mile you pass the stone gateway of **Gawlish Farm** and the track turns left. Go straight on through a gate into a green lane, following the public footpath sign. You now pass between high hedges fringed with wild flowers. After a short distance cross a stile into a field. Keep to the right and when the boundary turns right go straight on to another stile followed by a footbridge. Cross the next field to a gate into a lane and bear right.

The hedges along this stretch are filled with wild flowers in season – the primroses in spring are particularly good. Also look out for deer in the wood on the right.

Six hundred yards after joining the lane, you come to a junction; go straight on (signposted to Hartland Point and the lighthouse). The lane climbs and swings to the right.

At the top of the climb the lane swings left again. As it does so, you will see a public footpath sign pointing right up a track. To follow the *shorter version of the walk*, turn right here and follow the track past **East Titchberry Farm** and down to the **South West Coast Path** about 200 yards away. Turn right (see * below).

For the longer route, continue along the lane. It continues to wind, climbing occasionally, and soon you see **Hartland Point** ahead of you again. The radar dome is now on your right. The lane ends at **Blagdon Farm**. Go straight on along a track, and when you come to the farm buildings turn right, following the signpost for Hartland Point. Cross a stile and go down to join the **South West Coast Path**.

Turn left to go to the Hartland Point viewpoint, from which you can see the lighthouse, built in 1874, as well as enjoy extensive views, both to the south and to the east. On a clear day you can also see Lundy to the north. The strange structure on the right, which has been in view on and off for much of this first leg, is a radar dome, used for air traffic control.

Turn right onto the Coast Path, and climb up towards the dome. The

Drive and Stroll

The radar dome near Hartland Point

path now follows the cliff, winding into and out of farm fields. The general rule is to keep to the left in the fields, following the waymarks and the cliff edge. The views along this stretch are stunning, both along the coast and inland, where a patchwork of green fields stretches to the horizon. Follow the Coast Path for 2¼ miles (*1½ miles if you have chosen the shorter walk), until you are immediately opposite **East** and **West Fattacott**

Farms and come across a concrete triangulation point pillar on the left. Cross another three fields and you will see a Coast Path signpost (the first since the path from East Titchberry) just inside the fourth. Turn right and follow the hedge to a stile. Keep to the right of the next field to another stile, leading onto a track. Follow the track until it goes into a field; cross the stile on the left and follow a path back to the car park.

Places of Interest Nearby

Four miles to the east is the lovely heritage village of **Clovelly**. Telephone: 01237 431781. About the same distance away, on the other side of the A39, is the **Milky Way adventure park**. Telephone: 01237 431255.

Drive and Stroll

3 Buckland Brewer and Parkham

The 13th-century Coach and Horses at Buckland Brewer

The Walk 3¾ miles **Terrain** A few short climbs
Map OS Explorer 126 Clovelly and Hartland, and 139 Bideford, Ilfracombe and Barnstaple (GR 437209)

How to get there

Buckland Brewer is signposted south from the A39 Bideford to Bude road, and west from the A386 between Bideford and Torrington. **Parking**: There is parking along the road through the village.

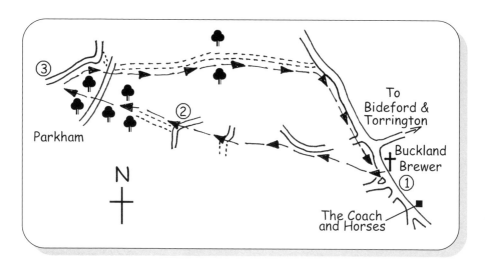

Introduction

Buckland Brewer is a small hilltop village in a quiet, peaceful part of Devon, a world away from the busy towns and holiday resorts on the coast to the north. Extensive views and hedge-fringed fields and lanes are the main features of this walk, although there are also a couple of delightful woodland stretches. The route takes you along paths and lanes to the neighbouring village of Parkham, and returns along a long green lane (there may be some muddy stretches). The hedgerows, especially those along the green lane, are filled with wild flowers in season (the spring primroses are particularly lovely), and the woods are full of birds.

The Coach and Horses

Just a short distance from the start of the walk, in Buckland Brewer, is this beautiful thatched 13th century coaching inn. It has the thick walls and low beams of the period, and the atmosphere is friendly and welcoming. There are four snug rooms: a bar and a lounge, both furnished with antique settles and tables, a games room, and a pretty, intimate little dining room. At the back is a delightful garden with a children's play area. The mouthwatering menu ranges from local pasties, sandwiches and jacket potatoes to a variety of main courses such as oven-baked sea bass and beef fillet with mushrooms. Seafood is a speciality, and their puddings are renowned. Telephone: 01237 451395. If you fancy a break in the middle of your walk, a short detour will take you the **Bell Inn** in Parkham, another delightful thatched pub, this time from the 14th century. Telephone: 01237 451201.

Drive and Stroll

THE WALK

The walk starts at the church, in the centre of the village. Opposite the tower you will see a public footpath sign pointing up a narrow path alongside a building. Follow that to some waste ground and then cross a stile into a field. Bear right to another little stile in an electric fence, and right again to a gate in the far corner. Cross the next field to another gate, which leads into a lane; turn left. Across the bank on your right you will get the first of the wonderful views on this walk.

The views you will get to the north from time to time along this whole route are outstanding. You look out over the rolling, green fields to the sea and across Bideford Bay. The headland you can see in the distance is Baggy Point, beyond Barnstaple.

After about 300 yards, as the lane swings right, go left through a gate, following the public footpath sign. Turn right on the other side and follow the right-hand hedge to a stile. Cross the next field, with the same lovely view to the right, aiming for the gap just to the right of the barn on the other side. Swing round to the right to a gate into a lane, and when it turns left and becomes a track go straight on to a sunken footpath, following the public footpath sign. Go through a gate on the right and cross the field to another stile (do not follow the left-hand boundary – that is a different path). Keep left in the next field to a gate leading into a lane; turn left.

After 100 yards, as the lane swings left, go straight on along a track, following the public footpath sign. It winds down between high banks and hedges, with a mass of wild flowers in season in the hedgerows alongside. Shortly before it ends at a gate, turn left into a wood, following the yellow waymark. Go down steeply to a stile, followed by a second, and cross a small footbridge. This is a pretty little wood, filled with birdsong.

Bear right after the footbridge and follow the path between banks as it climbs out of the valley to a stile. Cross a track to a gate and keep to the left of a field. A stile takes you into another lovely wood. Go steeply down to a road; when you reach it go left to a culvert under the road (you can go straight across the road, but there is a very steep bank opposite). On the other side, follow a path down to a stream. Go left and then right to cross a footbridge. Climb up to a stile leading into a field, and bear left on the other side to reach a gate and stile into a lane on the edge of the village of **Parkham**.

Turn left here for a slight detour into the village if you want to visit the

The valley near Parkham

Bell Inn. Otherwise turn right. There are more excellent views ahead and to the right. The lane twists to the right and to the left, descending as it goes. About 600 yards after joining the lane, look out for a track going off sharply to the right; follow it down to a bridge and on to the main road. Cross straight over to a surfaced track. This climbs out of the valley and becomes an unsurfaced green lane. At the top you get probably the best views of the walk. After ¼ mile you come to a junction; go straight on. Another ¼ mile further on cross a stream and the track forks; take the left fork, which becomes rougher with a tendency to be muddy. After another ½ mile or so you emerge onto a lane; turn right. At the T-junction ½ mile further on, bear right to return to the village.

Places of Interest Nearby

About 7 miles away, on the coast, is **Clovelly**, a beautifully preserved heritage village. Telephone: 01237 431781. On the way to it is the **Milky Way adventure park**. Telephone: 01237 431255. About 4 miles the other way, near Bideford, is the **Big Sheep theme park**. Telephone: 01237 472366.

4 The Two Moors Way at Knowstone

The Masons' Arms, Knowstone

The Walk 4¾ miles   **Terrain** Just one steep hill near the start
Map OS Explorer 114 Exeter and the Exe Valley (GR 827231)

How to get there

Knowstone is just over a mile north of the A361 between Tiverton and South Molton and is signposted from there. **Parking**: You can park alongside the road through the village.

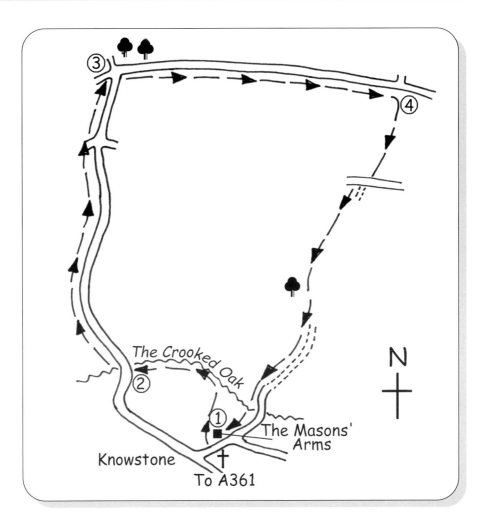

Introduction

The views along much of this route are outstanding, and the walk is worthwhile for them alone, but there is also a great deal more to appreciate: woods, streams, flowers, birds and a wide range of wildlife. It starts in the attractive, characterful village of Knowstone (pronounced 'nowstone') and follows quiet lanes for much of the way, but there are also pretty farm and woodland paths. The return leg is along the Two Moors Way (some parts of which may be muddy), a long-distance route that crosses Devon from Exmoor in the north to Dartmoor in the south.

Drive and Stroll

The Masons' Arms

This delightful thatched inn originated as a church house for the church across the road. The low doorway leads into a small bar, which has scrubbed pine tables, chairs and benches, and an enormous fireplace with a blazing fire in winter. Next door is a cosy dining area, which is similarly furnished with pine tables, but has a wood-burning stove instead of a fireplace. As you go through the arch leading to it, look out for the cigar-smoking fox's head above you! The thick walls and low beams throughout give the pub a snug feeling. Outside there is a terrace, with a lovely view over the valley. The food is outstanding, but be warned: pub snacks are not on offer; the menu is more akin to that of a restaurant than a traditional pub (with prices to match). Telephone: 01398 341231.

THE WALK

The walk starts on the main road through the village, between **St Peter's church** and the **Masons' Arms**.

Knowstone's main claim to fame is that it had the misfortune to be served by the Revd John Froude, who was vicar here from 1804 to 1853. A less Christian man would be hard to imagine. He was a great sportsman; he hunted three days a week, shot three days a week and held services when it pleased him – which was not often. He terrorised his neighbours, employing a bunch of thugs who burnt crops and mutilated livestock on his behalf. He so enraged his parishioners that one tried to murder him. He survived all attempts to remove him, however, and died in his bed aged 75.

Turn right from the pub and after a few yards right again through a gate,

following the public footpath sign. Cross a lawn to a stile and bear right on the other side to another stile. Bear half left to two more stiles in quick succession, leading into a wood. Follow the path that goes down to a stream (interestingly called the **Crooked Oak**) on the other side, swinging left as it does so.

It is very pretty with the **Crooked Oak** on your right and yellow gorse stretching up the hillside on your left. Go through a gate and then climb up the hill slightly to cross two stiles above some farm buildings. The path descends again and you emerge via another stile onto a lane; turn right.

Cross **Wadham Bridge** and follow the lane as it climbs out of the valley. As you do so, you get the first of the views, on the left along the valley to **Harpson Wood**. The lane then swings right and there is another view up ahead, this time across the undulating hills to **Exmoor**.

In addition to the birds in the hedgerows, there is a wealth of other wildlife to enjoy on this stretch. There seem to be pheasants in every field and hedge, the area is home to a large herd of red deer, and if you are lucky you might catch a glimpse of a fox. Further on, soon after you join the Two Moors Way you will also find some wild boar (although these hardly qualify as wildlife, as they are farmed).

After a mile you come to a crossroads. Go straight across (signposted to Molland). Another ¼ mile further on, at the next crossroads, turn right (signposted to Yeo Mill, Oldways End and East Anstey).

  (3)

You now have a pretty wood on your left and lush farmland on your right. After a while the wood gives way to hedges. The view to **Exmoor** over them and through gateways now stays with you as you follow this lane in an almost straight line for just over a mile.

  (4)

You will see a lane going left, signposted to Yeo Mill and Anstey, but look for a wooden fingerpost just before it, pointing right for the **Two Moors Way**. Leave the lane here and cross a stile. Keep to the left of a field to a gate and keep to the left again. Cross a stile at the end of that field and keep left to reach another stile leading into a road. Turn right and after 100 yards, turn left down a track at the signs for Whitefield and the **Two Moors Way**. The wild boar are on your left. At the end of the track, bear right to cross a footbridge and a stile and bear right across a field, following the Two Moors Way sign again. It can be a bit wet underfoot here after rain.

Cross another footbridge and bear right again to a gate. Keep to the left of the next field to a gate into a small wood and bear left. This stretch can also be muddy after rain. At the end of the wood, cross a clearing to a gate and follow the track on the other side. It bends right past a farm and then becomes a surfaced lane, which descends to cross the **Crooked Oak** and then swings right up a hill. At the T-junction at the top, turn right to return to the village.

Place of Interest Nearby

At South Molton, 8 miles away, is **Quince Honey Farm**, which has exhibitions and demonstrations. Telephone: 01769 572401.

5 The Torridge Valley through Beaford Wood

The countryside around Beaford

The Walk 2½ miles **Terrain** Easy going apart from two climbs
Map OS Explorer 127 South Molton and Chulmleigh (GR 553150)

How to get there

Beaford is on the A3124 between Exeter and Torrington. **Parking**: On the roads in the village.

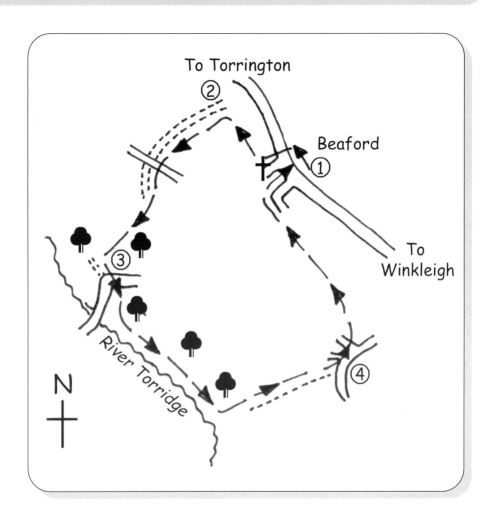

Introduction

Beaford is a very pretty village of cob and thatch, worth a brief exploration before venturing out to the surrounding fields and woodland. This route takes you initially across farmland and along green lanes, with extensive views over the surrounding countryside. It then descends to the valley of the majestic River Torridge, with its echoes of *Tarka the Otter*, and the delightful Beaford Wood, which is carpeted with flowers in the spring. After following the riverbank upstream for ½ mile, the walk climbs back out of the valley, and more farm paths bring you back to Beaford.

Drive and Stroll

The Royal Oak

Although there is a pub in Beaford, it does not serve food and even its range of liquid refreshment is somewhat restricted. My recommendation for refreshments, therefore, is the Royal Oak in Dolton, 2 miles away. It is a 16th century hostelry with an attractive, intimate bar, a snug, a delightful restaurant and a family room. It has a garden and children's play area at the back and tables on the square at the front, where you can watch the village go about its business. The menu is very varied, ranging from filled baguettes to steaks. Telephone: 01805 804288.

THE WALK

For ease of reference, these route directions start from outside the **Globe Inn** on the main road through **Beaford**. Turn right and then almost immediately left up a lane. After 100 yards you will see a public footpath sign pointing right through a gate; go through and to the right of some houses. Cross a stile into a field and bear slightly left. You immediately get a lovely view across the rolling countryside ahead of you. Climb another stile on the other side of the field and cross the next field to yet another stile leading into a green lane.

Turn left and follow the green lane between high, flower-filled banks. You come to a lane; cross over to a track. There is now another breathtaking view to the right and ahead across the **Torridge valley**. When you come to a house, go round to the right and through a gate into a field. Bear right to another gate and cross a field to a stile leading into a wood. Follow the path down to a track; turn left and almost immediately left again into a lane.

Follow the lane as it winds up a steepish hill. After about 100 yards you will see a public footpath sign pointing through a gate on the right; follow that. The path descends through the wood and then swings left past some houses to join the **River Torridge**.

The Torridge is wide and majestic at this point. It is probably best known as the playground of Tarka the otter in Henry Williamson's classic novel of that name. There is a long-distance route, the Tarka Trail, linking many of the places mentioned in the book, that passes to the west and south of this spot. Beaford Wood is alive with birdsong, and you will probably see some pheasants. It is particularly lovely in spring, when your path is surrounded by wild garlic, wood anemones and bluebells.

The majestic River Torridge

Follow the river upstream, crossing a footbridge over a small stream on the way. At the path junction on the other side, go straight on. About ½ mile after joining the river you will find a stile ahead of you. Do not cross it but follow the main path to the left and climb up out of the valley. You eventually leave the wood and join a track; bear left and continue to climb. Go through two gates onto a lane.

Go straight ahead and after 200 yards turn left down a small lane, following the public footpath sign. After another 50 yards turn right through a gate, again following a public footpath sign. Cross a field to the far corner, where you will be faced by three gates; take the left-hand one. Follow a track alongside a field on the other side, with another lovely view to your left. At the end go through the right-hand gate and follow a track between a fence and a hedge. Go through a kissing-gate and cross the next field to one last gate, which leads onto a road. Follow that and, at the end, cross over to a gate into a playground. Cross that to another gate into the churchyard. Turn right, leave the churchyard and follow the lane on the other side back to the main road in **Beaford**.

Beaford church

Places of Interest Nearby

About 5 miles from Beaford, near Great Torrington, are the Royal Horticultural Society's **Rosemoor Gardens**. Telephone: 01805 624067. In Torrington itself you can visit the **Dartington Crystal works**. Telephone: 01805 626262.

6 The Little Dart Valley

The Little Dart River at Yeo Copse

The Walk 3¾ miles   **Terrain** One fairly steep hill, otherwise easy
Map OS Explorer 114 Exeter and the Exe Valley (GR 803145)

How to get there

The walk starts at Witheridge, which is on the B3137 between Tiverton and South Molton. **Parking**: In The Square, in the middle of the village.

Drive and Stroll

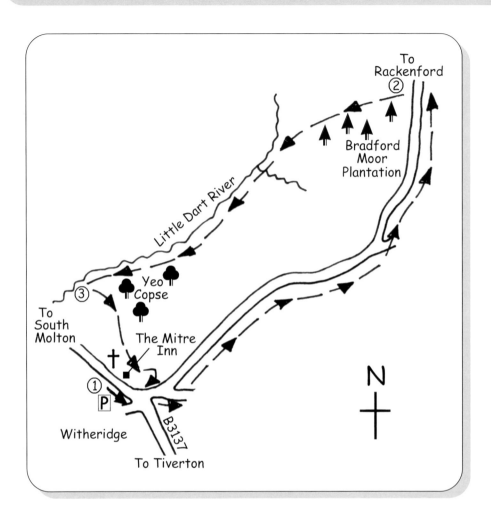

Introduction

Witheridge is an attractive upland village, with some interesting vernacular architecture – houses built of the local dark brown dunstone mingle with whitewashed cob and thatch cottages. This route follows quiet, hedge-fringed lanes north-east from the village centre to the headwaters of the Little Dart River, with good views over the rolling countryside. There it joins the Two Moors Way and follows this long-distance path alongside the river, through lovely meadows and into the pretty Yeo Copse. More farm paths bring you back to Witheridge.

The Mitre Inn

There are two pubs in Witheridge, both with their attractions, but for atmosphere my vote goes to this old coaching inn. Built of the local brown stone, it has a somewhat austere exterior, but the inside is warm and welcoming. To the left of the entrance is a cosy bar, decorated with old photographs and with a blazing log fire in the winter. Behind it is a small pool room. On the other side is a light, airy restaurant furnished with attractive pine tables and chairs. All the food is home cooked and the meat is all locally sourced. The menu ranges from chicken cakes to lasagne, steaks and fish dishes. Telephone: 01884 861263.

THE WALK

Turn east along the B3137 from The Square, away from the church. You will pass the Angel and Mitre pubs on either side of the road. After 200 yards or so turn left into a lane (signposted to the Parish Hall and Rackenford). Where the lane swings left at the edge of the village, follow it round, following the sign for Rackenford. The first of the views here is a lovely vista to the left and ahead across the verdant fields and woods. The lane descends to a stream and climbs up the other side of the valley. At the next junction, 700 yards beyond the stream, follow the main lane round to the left, following the sign for Rackenford again. After 500 or 600 yards, as the lane begins to descend again there is another extensive view ahead. Soon afterwards, you will see a footpath sign, with the **Two Moors Way** waymark, pointing left.

Turn off here and go through a gate and down a short track to a stile. Keep to the left of the boggy field beyond, alongside **Bradford Moor Plantation**.

The Two Moors Way is a long-distance route that runs from Ivybridge, on the southern edge of Dartmoor to Lynmouth on the Exmoor coast. As well as traversing the two moors, it also runs through some of the most attractive agricultural scenery in Devon. Along this stretch it follows the valley of the infant Little Dart River.

At the end of the plantation go through a gate and continue across the next field. It is beautifully peaceful along here, with only the birdsong to break the silence. A boardwalk takes you across a particularly boggy stretch and you then cross a footbridge and stile followed by another boardwalk. Cross a pretty meadow, with the

Drive and Stroll

The Mitre Inn offers a welcoming atmosphere

Little Dart on your right. Cross a stile at the end and cut straight across the next field. Follow the Two Moors Way waymark at the end to cross a stile and a footbridge. Bear right on the other side to a gate leading into the Woodland Trust's **Yeo Copse**. When the path forks on the other side go right to follow the river. This is a delightful stretch, with the wood on your left, the river gliding along to your right and the mill leat for **Witheridge Mill** alongside you. After 600 yards leave the copse and join a track.

 3

Turn left and climb to a gate. Keep to the right of the field on the other side. Towards the end, go through a gateway on the right and keep to the left of the next field. You can now see **Witheridge church** half right,

and there are lovely views behind you. Keep following the edge of the field round to the left until you reach the end. Here you rejoin the **Two Moors Way**; turn right. At the end of the field go through a kissing-gate and follow a grassy path alongside the parish hall. Another kissing-gate takes you into the lane you came out on. Turn right and at the T-junction right again to return to the centre of **Witheridge**.

Places of Interest Nearby

About 10 miles away, at South Molton, is **Quince Honey Farm**, which has exhibitions and demonstrations. Telephone: 01769 572401. About the same distance the other way, near Tiverton, is the National Trust's **Knightshayes Court**. Telephone: 01884 254665.

7 | Dunkeswell

The Royal Oak is a 16th century coaching inn

The Walk 3 miles   **Terrain** Fairly hilly but generally not too strenuous
Map OS Explorer 115 Exmouth and Sidmouth (GR 140077)

How to get there

Turn north off the A30 at Honiton, following the signs for the A35, and then turn right after 200 yards and follow the signs for Dunkeswell. **Parking**: The best places to park are in the pull-in opposite the Royal Oak on the main road or opposite the village hall on the lane into the village centre.

Drive and Stroll

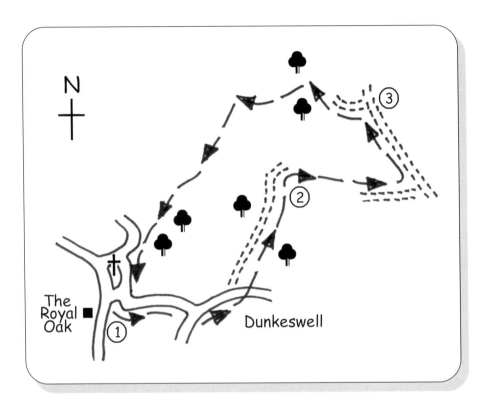

Introduction

This varied walk takes you through the pretty village of Dunkeswell, with its thatched and slate-roofed houses and cottages, and up the valley of the Madford River. There are good views to enjoy from the higher ground, some lovely woods to amble through, and a wealth of wild flowers in season in the fields and hedgerows. There are some hills to climb, but nothing too strenuous, and also some wet or muddy stretches after rain, so go suitably shod.

The Royal Oak

The Royal Oak is a lovely 16th century coaching inn, where a warm welcome awaits visitors. The main bar has a wooden floor with tables, chairs, upholstered stools and window seats. Off it is a delightful snug furnished with deep armchairs. Between the two is a large stone fireplace with a wood-burning stove, which serves both rooms. The stone walls and small windows give it a cosy, warm atmosphere. Along a short passage is a large, part-tiled, part-carpeted restaurant. There are also tables outside. They offer traditional pub food, ranging from sandwiches and jacket potatoes to steak and fish, and a three-course restaurant menu. Telephone: 01404 891683.

THE WALK

If you have parked opposite the **Royal Oak**, follow the road up for a short distance to a lane on the right, signposted to the village hall. Follow it past the hall to a junction and turn right. The lane descends steeply and swings to the left. It then bends right and climbs through some trees to a T-junction; turn left. After 200 yards the lane swings right; go straight on down a surfaced track. You pass some houses and get a good view half left. When the main track goes right into a farmyard, bear left down a hill through a small wood.

About 500 yards after leaving the lane, the track forks; go straight on. You now have a stream tumbling along to your left. When the track swings left through a gate, go straight on up some steps, following the yellow waymark. Go through a barrier and follow the path on the other side through the trees, alongside a fence, to a stile. Go straight across the field on the other side and cross a stream – the River Madford. Continue up the field,

which can become a bit muddy, aiming for the far right-hand corner. At the top you will find a small gate on the right; go through it onto a drive. Turn left and follow it up to a gate; turn left again, onto a surfaced track.

The village pump, Dunkeswell

The church of St Nicholas, Dunkeswell

✎ ③

After 500 yards there is a fork; follow the main track round to the left. You descend to a stream; cross a footbridge and go through a small gate. Turn right on the other side and keep following the yellow waymarks past a house to another gate. Turn left on the other side and go through a gate into a wood. Follow the path up a hill and leave the wood via another gate. Be careful along here as it can be a bit boggy. Follow the path alongside a fence and go through a gate onto a green lane. When that swings to the left, bear right, following the blue waymark. At the top you come to a track; bear left to a gate. On the other side, turn right, following the blue waymark.

After 50 yards or so, look out for a post on the left with a yellow waymark; follow it through a gate and keep to the right of the field on the other side. Cross a stile and keep to the right again. You now get a good view to the left. Go through a gate at the end into a farmyard. Follow a track out of the yard and to the right. When it swings right again, following the right-hand boundary of a field, go left through a gate and follow the left-hand side of the field, with a hedge on your left and an electric fence on your right. After 200 yards go through a kissing-gate on the left and follow the path along the top of a wood. At the end, go through another kissing-gate onto a lane; turn left. At the junction, turn left, following the sign for **Dunkeswell**. Pass the church and at the next junction follow the main lane round to the right to the village hall and the main road.

Place of Interest Nearby

Five miles away, in Honiton, is the **Allhallows Museum**, which has displays about the lace for which the town is famous. Telephone: 01404 44966.

8 | Shobrooke and Trew Woods

The beautiful view from Trew Woods

The Walk 4½ miles   **Terrain** Generally easy, with just a few gentle climbs
Map OS Explorer 114 Exeter and the Exe Valley (GR 866013)

How to get there

Shobrooke is just east of the A3072 Crediton to Tiverton road and is signposted from both directions. **Parking**: Customers may park in the Red Lion's car park (but please ask first). Otherwise there is parking by the roadside.

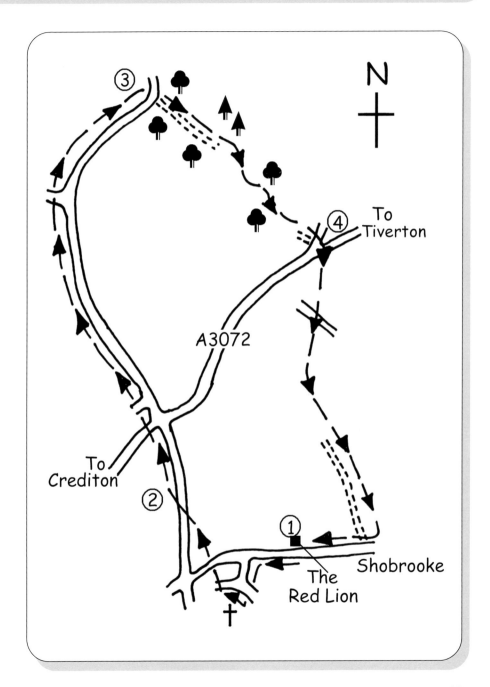

N

③

④ To Tiverton

A3072

To Crediton

②

① Shobrooke

The Red Lion

Drive and Stroll

Introduction

This is a delightful corner of Devon, close to the bustle of Crediton yet enclosed in a tranquil world of its own, and the walk shows it at its best. There is a great deal of variety along the route, ranging from quiet little lanes to cool woodland paths, and from wild flowers in the hedgerows to stunning views across the surrounding hills and woods. It is quite long, but nowhere is the going difficult.

The Red Lion Inn

This friendly, welcoming hostelry comprises three rooms: a plain bar and games room on the left as you go in, a comfortable lounge with an open fire in winter on the right, and behind it a light, airy dining area. Outside there is a pretty beer garden and patio, and a children's play area, all with a lovely view across the countryside. The food ranges from soups and salads to pasta and fish dishes and such mouthwatering delights as 'smothered chicken'. Telephone: 01363 772340.

THE WALK

Turn right from the Red Lion, and after 50 yards go left up some steps. Go through a gate and bear right across a field. As you go you get a good view across the hills and woods on the left. At the end cross a stile into a lane; turn left. At the T-junction, turn right, passing **Shobrooke church** on your left. After 100 yards, go right up some steps and through a kissing-gate into a field. Bear left to another kissing-gate leading into a lane. Cross over and cross a stile into another field. Go straight across to a gate into a lane. (If the field is planted with crops and there is no path across it, as is sometimes the case, then turn left at the lane and right at the first crossroads to meet up with the route at the end of the field.)

Bear right in the lane. You now get another lovely view to your right. After 350 yards you come out at the A3072; cross it, following the sign for Stockleigh English. The views stay with you, both to left and right, through gaps in the hedges, and the banks are full of a variety of wild flowers in season. The lane climbs gently. After ¾ mile you come to a junction; go straight on (signposted to Stockleigh English and Cheriton Fitzpaine). Another ½ mile further on, as the lane swings sharp left, turn right through a gateway onto a track.

After a few yards the track swings

40

The Red Lion extends a friendly welcome

right; go left down another track into **Trew Woods**. The track is a mass of the herb self-heal in summer. When it ends at a pair of solid wooden gates, bear left along a path, following the yellow waymark. Look out for deer along here. The path broadens to a track; soon after it does so, watch out for a post with a yellow waymark pointing along a narrower path up the hill to the right. At the top of the climb you come to another track; turn left into a conifer plantation. When the main track goes left down the hill, go straight on along another track, following the yellow waymark. You are now running along the edge of the wood and soon come out onto a gravel track; bear left.

Just before you get to a house, go through a gate on the left, following the yellow waymark again. Go down a steep slope, cross a valley and turn right on the other side, following a path along the edge of a wood. About halfway down, you will find a gate on the left leading into the wood. Go through and follow the broad path on the other side. At the end go through a gate and turn left to follow the edge of a field. Follow the hedge round to the right at the end and you will come to a gate on

41

the left. Go through it and keep to the left of the field. At the end, a track leads down to a farmyard and a lane.

Turn right and after a few yards you come to the A3072 again. Cross over to a stile and cross the field on the other side to another stile in the far left-hand corner, leading into a lane; turn left. After a few yards, just before you get to the bridge across **Shobrooke Lake** turn right across another stile and cross the field beyond (do not take the path to the right). There is a gap in the trees on the other side, marked with a post and a yellow waymark. Cross the next field to two footbridges and two stiles in quick succession. Keep to the right of a field to a stile in the corner, and cross the next field. Follow the bank on the other side to the left and cross a stile. On the other side you join a track; follow it across another field and through a farmyard. It ends at a lane in **Shobrooke**; turn right to return to the pub.

Place of Interest Nearby

About 9 miles away is **Exeter**, with its beautiful cathedral, museums and old city walls.

---

9 | Ashclyst Forest

The view from Ashclyst Forest

The Walk 2 miles   **Terrain** Generally level, easy paths and tracks
Map OS Explorer 115 Exmouth and Sidmouth (GR 999993)

How to get there

Turn east off the B3181 at Budlake, north of Broadclyst, following the sign for Caddihoe and Ashclyst Forest. Follow the road into the forest. **Parking**: Park at the Forest Gate car park, more or less in the centre of the forest.

Drive and Stroll

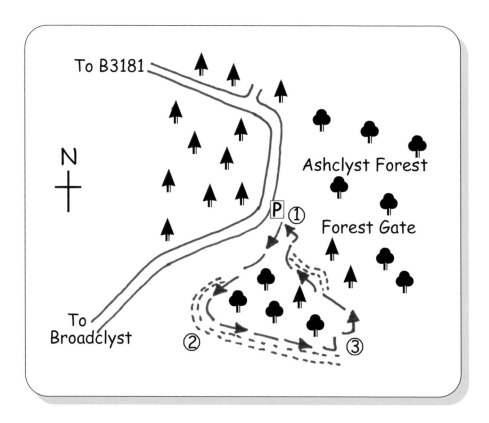

To B3181

N

Ashclyst Forest

Forest Gate

P ①

To Broadclyst

②   ③

Introduction

Ashclyst Forest is owned by the National Trust, and is part of the Killerton estate. It is a lovely area of mixed woodland, some ancient, some fairly recent, most of it deciduous but with some areas of conifers. This easy amble follows clear, waymarked paths and tracks down to its southern boundary, where there are lovely views over the farmland, and back. There is a wealth of wild flowers to enjoy along the way, plus some interesting wildlife.

The Red Lion Inn

You will find this welcoming 15th century pub alongside the church in Broadclyst, 1½ miles away. It is full of character, with low beams and enormous stone fireplaces in both of its main rooms. The lounge is carpeted and furnished with pews and tables and chairs, and there is a wood-burning stove in its fireplace; the one in the flagstoned bar to the rear has an open fire. Outside is a cobbled patio overlooking the church, and there is a pretty garden across the lane. The food is good country fare, ranging from baps and jacket potatoes to steak and kidney pie, fresh Brixham fish and a mouthwatering array of daily specials. Telephone: 01392 461271.

THE WALK

From the information board in the centre of the car park, follow the red signpost. When you get to the edge of the car park, you will see a path going right, with a red-marked post alongside. Turn along here.

Ashclyst Forest was originally a mixture of ancient woodland, fields and open land, criss-crossed by medieval tracks and roads. In the 19th century, Sir Thomas Acland planted many of the fields and downs with trees, creating the forest you see today. You can still see traces of its history in the hedge banks that delineated the original woodland and the old tracks that led to it.

You pass through an area of mixed woodland, with broadleaved trees on the left and conifers on the right. The path goes to the left and the right and you come to a track; go straight on across it. Cross a hedge bank and enter an open stretch, which is a mass of foxgloves in the summer, with marsh thistles to add variety. At the end of the open ground, the track you are following goes straight on; you should turn left along a path into the woods, following the red waymark. Pass a barrier and join a track; go straight on.

The track soon swings left and follows the edge of the forest. You now have a hedge bank on your right, with some lovely views out across the countryside.

There is a great deal to interest the naturalist along this stretch of the forest. Among the flowers you will come across in the early summer is the beautiful early purple orchid, and a bit later dog roses and hedge woundwort. You might also see a buzzard swooping low along the paths or soaring high above the trees, and there are pheasants and roe deer. The forest is a nationally important site for butterflies, and one of the main species to be seen in early summer is the pearl bordered fritillary.

After some distance, the track forks; go straight on along the edge of the forest. At the next junction, where there is a path going left, follow the

Drive and Stroll

Ashclyst Forest is owned by the National Trust

main path round to the right, still keeping to the edge of the wood.

  3

At the next path junction, go left, following the red waymark. This stretch is lined with dog roses and sweet-smelling privet. At the next junction, follow the clear path to the right in a U-turn, and then to the left. You are now among conifers. You come to a T-junction; turn right. When you come to a gate, go round it and straight on along a broad track. After 100 yards or so, turn right onto a path, following the red arrow. After a short distance go round a barrier and you will find yourself back in the car park.

Places of Interest Nearby

The National Trust's **Killerton House** is about 2 miles away. Telephone: 01392 881345. Seven miles away is **Exeter**, with its cathedral, museums and ancient city walls.

10 The East Devon Way at Sidbury

View from the lovely Core Hill Wood

The Walk 4¾ miles   **Terrain** Some steep hills
Map OS Explorer 115 Exmouth and Sidmouth (GR 139918)

How to get there

Sidbury is on the A375 Sidmouth to Honiton road, just north of Sidmouth. **Parking**: In the free car park towards the northern end of the village.

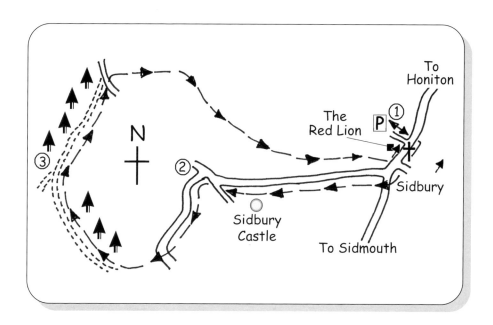

Introduction

Sidbury is a delightful village set in amazingly beautiful countryside. After a brief exploration of the village, this walk takes you along hedge-fringed lanes up to lovely Core Hill Wood, passing the Iron Age hill fort of Sidbury Castle as you go. There are some excellent views along the way. You follow a track through the wood to join the East Devon Way, from which the views across the valley of the River Sid are stunning. After some more woodland rambling, you return to Sidbury via farm paths and tracks, keeping the view across the valley ahead of you for most of the way. There are some steep climbs before you can enjoy the views, but the paths and tracks are very clear.

The Red Lion Inn

The rather plain exterior of this pub belies the warm welcome you will receive inside, from both the landlady and the locals. The accommodation comprises two rooms: a friendly bar, partly carpeted, decorated with old photographs and with a large brick fireplace, and an airy dining room. The latter leads into a courtyard, which is a real suntrap. The food is all home made and ranges from jacket potatoes, sandwiches and salads to specials such as steak, cauliflower cheese and the fresh fish for which the inn is renowned. Telephone: 01395 597313.

Drive and Stroll

Turn right as you leave the car park, and at the T-junction after a few yards turn right again into the main street. Pass **St Giles's church** on the left.

This unusual church is worth a visit. The crypt is Saxon, but was only discovered in 1898, as it was filled in when the chancel was built. The chancel itself and the tower date from the 12th century, and there was further reconstruction work done in the 15th and 17th centuries.

Pass the **Red Lion** and follow the road round to the right. Just by the **War Memorial**, turn right up a lane called **Greenhead**. This takes you out of the village and up a hill. As you climb, look to the right for the first of a series of lovely views, across the fields and woods. Towards the top of the climb you pass a steep hill on the left, at the top of which is **Sidbury Castle**.

Sidbury Castle is an Iron Age hill fort, which consists of an earth rampart, a ditch, and a bank. It was a defensive structure, intended to protect the inhabitants – and often other people from the surrounding area, who owed allegiance to the same chief and would come into the fort in times of trouble – from attack.

It is, however, on private land and there is no public access.

At the T-junction at the top, follow the main lane round to the right (signposted to Ottery St Mary). You now get a superb view ahead of you and to the right.

 (2)

After about 100 yards, turn left down another lane (signposted to Burscombe Farm). Follow this lane down steeply into a valley, and then up equally steeply on the other side. As the main lane swings left at the top, go straight on up some steps to a stile, following the public footpath sign. Go straight across the field on the other side to reach the lovely **Core Hill Wood**. You will find a metal gate on your left; go through it and turn immediately right along the edge of the wood.

Continue to climb, and when you get to the top you will find a path junction; turn right and then after a few yards sharp left to follow a gully downhill. The path curves round to the right and you come to a gap in a fence, leading onto a track; turn right. The track climbs again through the wood to a stretch of open ground, which is covered in purple heather and yellow gorse in late summer. Re-enter the wood, and through the trees you now get a magnificent view to the right. When you come to a junction, bear right along the main track.

The church of St Giles, Sidbury

Drive and Stroll

⤷ (3)

You are now on the **East Devon Way**, a 38-mile walking and riding trail that runs from Exmouth to Lyme Regis. Ignore tracks going off to left and right, keeping to the main track along the top of the hill. When that swings left a little over ½ mile further on, go straight on. Cross a lane and follow a short track to a stile. Cross it and turn right in the field beyond. Aim to the left of the wooded valley ahead of you. You now have another stunning view across the valley of the **River Sid**.

Cross a stile and keep to the right of the next field, just above the valley. Go through a gap in a hedge, and just before you get to the bank at the end of the next field bear right, following the yellow waymark.

Go down the field and through a gateway onto a rough track; bear left. The track narrows to a grassy path between hedges. Go through a gate at the end onto a track by a house; go straight on. After 200 yards, as the track bears right, look out for a stile on the left marked with the pink **East Devon Way** waymark. Cross it and turn right on the other side. Keep to the right of a field to a stile and turn left on the other side. Follow the edge of the field round, and at the end go through a gateway. Follow a track down to another gate, and then to a surfaced drive. Cross that to a surfaced lane, and where it ends go straight on along another track. This leads you back to the main road in **Sidbury**; turn left for the pub and the car park.

Places of Interest Nearby

About 5 miles east along the coast is **Branscombe**, where you will find the Old Bakery, Manor Mill and the Forge, all owned by the National Trust, with the last two restored to working order. Telephone: 01297 680333, 01392 881691 and 01297 680481 respectively. Six miles to the west are the lovely gardens of **Bicton Park**. Telephone: 01395 568465.

11 The Two Castles Trail and Lew Wood

Sabine Baring-Gould's medieval cross shaft, Lew Mill

The Walk 4¾ miles   **Terrain** Two steady but not difficult climbs
Map OS Explorer 112 Launceston and Holsworthy (GR 457861)

How to get there

The walk starts at the hamlet of Lewtrenchard, south of the A30 Okehampton to Launceston road. If you are coming from the west, turn off at Liftondown, from the east turn off at Sourton. In both cases follow the signs for Lewdown; when you get there turn south, following the sign for Lewtrenchard. **Parking**: On the road outside the church.

Drive and Stroll

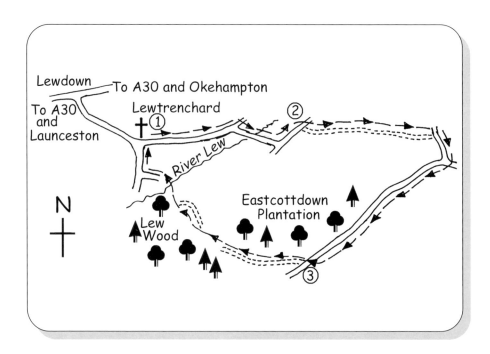

Introduction

An interesting and varied walk that explores the world of the Revd Sabine Baring-Gould, a 19th century scholar and a local figure of some note. Along the way, you follow part of the Two Castles Trail, enjoy extensive views in every direction (including two moors), and pass through pretty Lew Wood. There is one steady climb on the outward leg and another on the way back, but neither is particularly onerous and the route is otherwise very easy.

The Harris Arms

This 16th century coaching inn is at Portgate, about 2¾ miles west of Lewtrenchard. It comprises one long bar, with a large stone fireplace at one end and a wood-burning stove at the other. At the back is a light, airy eating area, and outside you will find a beer garden with breathtaking views across the rolling fields to Dartmoor. The pub has won several awards for its food, which is all home cooked and ranges from soup and ploughman's lunches to a mouthwatering array of main courses, including locally reared beef and pork, fresh fish and vegetarian dishes. They are also known for their wines and real ales. Telephone: 01566 783331.

THE WALK

Turn left from **St Peter's church**, where the Revd Sabine Baring-Gould was rector for many years, and follow the lane past **Lewtrenchard Manor**, once his home and now a hotel.

Sabine Baring-Gould was squire here for 47 years and rector for 43 years at the end of the 19th century and the beginning of the 20th. He was a man of many parts, but is perhaps best known as the author of the hymn Onward Christian Soldiers. *He also collected the folk stories and songs of Devon – including* Widecombe Fair. *He was an eccentric man: before coming to Lewtrenchard he was a teacher, and was noted for conducting his lessons with his pet bat on his shoulder!*

You soon enter a wood, and after 250 yards or so pass a public bridleway going left, waymarked as the Baring-Gould Trail. Go straight on along the lane, following the **Two Castles Trail** waymark.

The Two Castles Trail is a 24-mile route which links the castles of Okehampton and Launceston, now both ruined and in the hands of English Heritage.

Continue along the lane for another ½ mile until you come to a junction; turn right (signposted to Lew Mill). Follow this new lane down past some houses; the one on the left was the **Dower House** for Lewtrenchard Manor. The large stone in front of it is a medieval cross shaft erected there by Baring-Gould. At the bottom of the hill the lane crosses the **River Lew**. At the junction beyond the river, follow the main lane round to the left.

St Peter's church, Lewtrenchard

The dovecote at Lewtrenchard Manor

After 200 yards pass the entrance to Galford Springs Country Club. Just beyond it, turn right into the gateway of **Galford Farm**, following the **Two Castles Trail** waymark. Follow the drive to the left to two gates, and continue along the broad track on the other side. It climbs steadily, but towards the top you are rewarded with a superb view to your left. When the main track turns right, go straight on along a less clear track to a gate. Bear left along the next field and you soon get a good view towards **Dartmoor**. You now have a magnificent panorama, with **Bodmin Moor** in the distance behind you, Dartmoor ahead and a rolling patchwork of woods and fields to the left.

The track takes you to a gate on the right. Bear left on the other side to a stile. Turn right in the lane on the other side. At the T-junction turn right again (signposted to Coryton). You have now left the Two Castles Trail. As you follow this lane you have **Eastcottdown Plantation** on your right and another superb view over to your left, with **Brent Tor** and its church standing out on the horizon. After 1 mile you will find a track on the right leading into the wood, with a public footpath sign.

Turn off the lane here and follow the track. At the fork, continue along the main track (the lower one). At the next fork go right to climb through the wood. At the top, you come to another track; cross straight over to a narrow path through trees and bracken to a gate. Cross a field to the angle of the wood on the other side. There you will find a stile; cross it into **Lew Wood**. Turn left and then right, following the yellow waymark. Go down to a track and turn right, again following the yellow waymark. Go steeply down to meet another track and turn right and immediately left. After a couple of hundred yards you come to a path going right marked with the **Baring-Gould Trail** waymark; take that. Go through a kissing-gate and across a field to a footbridge. Go through a small stretch of woodland on the other side to a track; turn right and the track soon becomes a surfaced lane. Follow this to a T-junction and turn right again along a road, which brings you back to the church.

Place of Interest Nearby

About 3 miles away, towards Lifton, is **Dingles Steam Village**, a display of a variety of working steam engines. Telephone: 01566 783425.

12 | Bovey Valley Woods

Hisley Bridge is a stone packhorse bridge

The Walk 4 miles   **Terrain** Just a couple of short climbs
Map OS Explorer OL28 Dartmoor (GR 788801)

How to get there

Turn west off the A382 at Bovey Tracey and follow the B3387. At the fork just outside the town, go right, following the sign for Manaton. About a mile beyond the fork, turn right, following the sign for Lustleigh. At the bottom of the hill, just before a bridge, turn left into the Pullabrook Wood car park. **Parking**: In the free Woodland Trust car park.

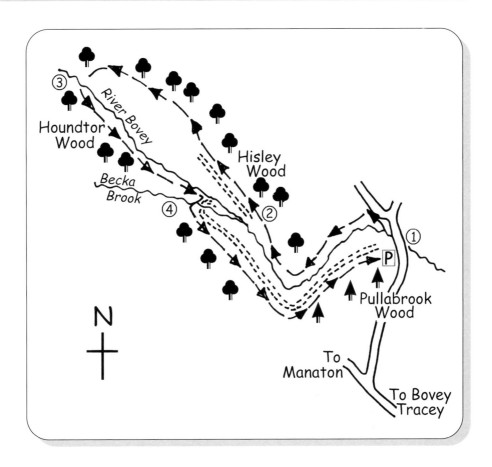

Introduction

The three Bovey Valley woods (Pullabrook, Hisley and Houndtor) are an absolute delight to wander through. Most of the area is managed by the Woodland Trust, and what is not is managed by English Nature. This walk sticks close to the River Bovey along one of its most attractive stretches for much of the route, and its chatter is a constant accompaniment to your amble. This is an all-year walk, with spring and summer flowers in abundance and the autumn colours are quite magnificent. Even in winter, the bare trees have a charm of their own.

The Kestor Inn

This is a fairly modern hostelry at Manaton, about 2¾ miles away. It has a large bar divided into snug alcoves and areas, furnished with upholstered bench seats and with a wood-burning stove at one end. There is also a family room and a lovely restaurant with large picture windows overlooking the garden and woods. Outside is a beer garden with a children's play area. The food is all home made (including the bread for the sandwiches), and includes soup, fish cakes and a range of main course specials. Telephone: 01647 221204.

THE WALK

Go back down the short track from the car park, and at the lane turn left to cross a bridge over the **River Bovey**. After 100 yards or so you will come to a junction; turn left. After another 150 yards, go through a gate on the left into a field. Cross the field to another gate, which leads you into **Hisley Wood**.

The flowers along here are a picture. The area to the right is carpeted with bluebells in spring, interspersed with greater stitchwort; a little later come red campion, yellow rattle, pink purslane and many more.

The path meanders alongside the river for about ¾ mile to **Hisley Bridge**, a lovely stone packhorse bridge on the left.

It then becomes a track and climbs away from the river (signposted to Lustleigh and Hisley). At the junction at the top, go straight on (signposted to Lustleigh). At the next junction follow the main track up the hill, following the path sign. When the track turns sharp right go straight on along a path to a stile. On the other side, follow the path to the right. At the junction, go left (signposted to Manaton via Water). At the next junction go straight on (signposted to Manaton via Water again). The path now takes you down to the left, back to the river at the interesting **Clam Bridge**, a log footbridge.

On the other side of the bridge turn left to follow the river downstream through **Houndtor Wood**.

The river here is at its most attractive, tumbling and cascading over enormous moss-covered boulders, rocks and fallen trees. The woods are also alive with birdsong, and after a while you will be able to see the bracken-covered open moor stretching up the side of the valley to the right.

The path takes you high up above the river again, with whortleberries on either side. After about ¾ mile, it swings right and becomes a track.

The River Bovey rushes beneath Clam Bridge, a log footbridge

You now follow the Becka Brook, a tributary of the Bovey, upstream for a short distance. Then the track swings left to cross a bridge.

On the other side, turn left along another track (signposted to Trendlebere Down). This track runs a little distance away from the brook and then the river and then begins to climb. Near the top of the hill, about ½ mile after crossing the Becka Brook, you will see a large cleared area on the left, separated from the track by a bank. Cross it to a gate leading into **Pullabrook Wood**. Follow the track on the other side and where it forks, go right. At the next fork, keep left to descend gently to a gate. The car park is on the other side.

Places of Interest Nearby

About 2½ miles away, towards Manaton, is the beauty spot and animal centre of **Becky Falls**. Telephone: 01647 221259. About the same distance the other way, at Bovey Tracey, you will find the **Devon Guild of Craftsmen's Riverside Centre**. Telephone: 01626 832223.

13 Cox Tor and the Staple Tors

The moors from Cox Tor

The Walk 3 miles   **Terrain** Open moorland with virtually no climbing (unless you choose to do so)
Map OS Explorer OL28 Dartmoor (GR 539750)

How to get there

The walk starts just west of Merrivale on the B3357 between Princetown and Tavistock. **Parking**: There is a car park on the northern side of the road at the top of the hill to the west of Merrivale. (Note: there are three car parks on the open moor between Merrivale and Tavistock; the walk starts at the easternmost one.)

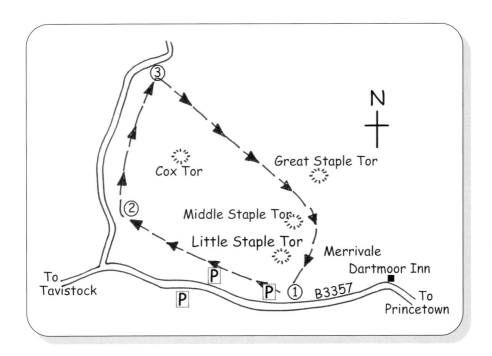

Introduction

This walk shows you Dartmoor at its very best: rolling moorland stretching out in every direction, a vast sky above you and superb views which can be enjoyed without very much climbing (although if you are prepared to tackle Cox Tor, the panorama will take your breath away). Along the way, there is the chance to explore some ancient tin workings. This is open moorland, and there are no marked paths. You can walk where you want; the route description is therefore more of a guide than a prescription.

The Dartmoor Inn

This well-preserved, 17th century hostelry is at the bottom of the hill to the east of the car park. It comprises a long lounge bar, with an enormous granite fireplace at one end, and a snug public bar leading off it. The lounge has an interesting collection of china, some of it hanging from the beams. There are also tables outside, with lovely views across the River Walkham. The pub is known for its country wines, and for the quality of its food, which ranges from ploughman's lunches, salads and soups to main courses such as lasagne and steak. Telephone: 01822 890340.

Drive and Stroll

THE WALK

Face away from the road and bear left across the moor. There is no set path, but as long as you walk roughly parallel to the road but slightly away from it, you will be going in the right direction. In summer you may prefer to keep closer to the road to avoid a large patch of bracken, but you should always be able to find a path through it. You will soon see a large tor looming up ahead of you; that is **Cox Tor**, and you should aim for it. In late summer you will be surrounded by purple heather and yellow gorse.

Cox Tor is one of hundreds of tors on Dartmoor. They were formed millennia ago by eruptions of molten magma, which rose from under the earth's crust without breaking the surface. As the softer soils above it eroded away, these strange outcrops of granite were left dotted across the landscape.

You have to go down into a gully, cross a small stream and climb out on the other side. All around you as you do so, are the remains of ancient tin workings.

Tin might well have been mined as early as the Bronze Age, although the first records date from the medieval period. At that time the tinners scoured streams like this one for the valuable ore. As the stream beds were worked out, the miners diverted the water slightly, resulting in wide gullies such as this. As you cross it you will see a number of mounds; these are the spoil tips onto which the miners threw any waste soil and stones. Most of them have become covered in vegetation over the centuries. Elsewhere on the moor you will come across deep gullies called girts cut into hillsides; these were formed when the miners started digging into the slopes, following the lodes of ore up from the valleys.

You now get a magnificent view to your left, all the way to Plymouth and the River Tamar. The route shown on the sketch map skirts **Cox Tor**, but if you are feeling more energetic you can climb the tor for a 360 degree panorama that will take your breath away.

If you are skirting the tor, swing right soon after passing it, to head north. Just before you do, you begin to get another lovely view ahead of you, all the way into Cornwall on a clear day. Below you on the left as you go round you will see a small road. Continue parallel to it (or, if you are right at the bottom of the slope, along it).

When the road joins a wall and then swings left, you should bear right along the northern side of **Cox Tor**.

The panoramic views from Cox Tor are spectacular

You now get a superb view to your left – apart from one or two farms in the valley immediately below you, there is no sign of human habitation, just the empty moors stretching away to the horizon. You will see a range of tors ahead of you, and behind them the mast on **North Hessary Tor**, just outside Princetown. You should head between **Middle Staple Tor**, which is to the right of the mast, and the larger **Great Staple Tor**, which is almost in front of it. Go round Middle Staple Tor and turn right again immediately beyond it. You now have the same view ahead of you that you had at the start of the walk. Pass **Little Staple Tor** on your right and soon you will see the car park by the road. Head straight down to it.

Place of Interest Nearby

At Princetown, 2½ miles away is the **High Moorland Visitor Centre**, with displays and exhibitions about Dartmoor. Telephone: 01822 890414.

14 Stover Lake and the Templer Way

Stover Lake is a haven for water birds

The Walk 5 miles   **Terrain** Mainly on level paths
Map OS Explorer 110 Torquay and Dawlish (GR 833750)

How to get there

Stover Country Park is on the A382 between Newton Abbot and Bovey Tracey. **Parking**: In the country park pay-and-display car park.

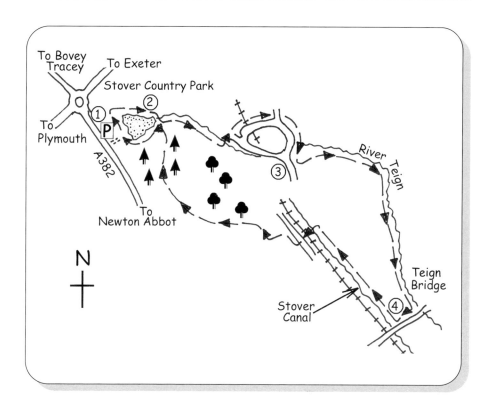

Introduction

This delightfully varied walk combines a lake, woods, farm fields, a river and a disused canal, with a wealth of flora and fauna to enjoy along the way. It starts at Stover Country Park, a nature reserve run by Devon County Council. The lake at its centre is full of water birds. You then meander through the surrounding wood, following the Templer Way, which runs from Dartmoor to the sea. Farm paths take you across to the River Teign, and after following that downstream across more farm fields, you trace the route of the Stover Canal (now largely filled in). After more woodland paths, you will find yourself back at Stover Lake.

The Old Thatched Inn

This pretty 17th century coaching inn in Bovey Tracey, 2½ miles away, has been very well preserved. It comprises three rooms: a bar, a dining room and a games room. There is a large chimney between the bar and the dining

Drive and Stroll

room, with stone fireplaces on both sides. A pleasant beer garden at the rear completes the accommodation. The food is good standard bar food, and ranges from ploughman's lunches and sandwiches to a range of mouthwatering main courses. Telephone: 01626 833421.

THE WALK

Make your way down to the lake, going to the left of the interpretation centre, and turn left. You soon leave the lake and follow a stream for a short distance to a footbridge.

Stover Lake is a haven for water birds. Among the ducks on view are mallard, pochard, crested duck and grebe, and there are also swans, coots and moorhens on the water. The area is home to a wide variety of insect and amphibian life.

After crossing the footbridge, turn right and return to the bank of the lake. Follow it for about ¼ mile to a track.

Turn right across another bridge, and on the other side turn left, away from the lake, to follow the **Templer Way** down **Ventiford Brook**.

The Templer Way is named after George Templer, who lived at Stover (the country park is part of his estate, although the house is now a school). He owned the Haytor Quarry on Dartmoor, which supplied granite for some of London's major Victorian public buildings, including the National Gallery and the British Museum. The way follows the route along which the granite was transported on its way to the sea at Teignmouth.

The path follows the brook through the wood, and soon you will see a footbridge leading to a road ahead. Just before you reach it, turn right, following the Templer Way waymark. At the junction go straight on. Eventually you will see the edge of the wood ahead and a Templer Way waymark will direct you to the right. Go through a kissing-gate onto a road and turn right, then immediately left down **Summer Lane**. Follow that round to the right to cross a railway line. At the T-junction turn right, and after 300 yards follow the lane round to the right to another T-junction.

Turn left and after 100 yards you cross a bridge; turn left immediately on the other side down a track, following the Templer Way sign. Go through a gate into a field and at the end go through another kissing-gate. Keep to the left, with the **River Teign** alongside you, across more fields. You will pass two footbridges across the river, and a sign directing

The aerial walkway at Stover Lake

the Templer Way to the left; ignore them all and continue alongside the river for about 1¼ mile to a kissing-gate leading into a road. Turn right and follow the road for 300 yards until you see a path on the right just before a bridge, signposted as the **Templer Way**.

  ④

Cross two stiles and follow the path alongside the remains of the **Stover Canal**.

The Stover Canal was constructed towards the end of the 18th century to carry ball clay from the Bovey valley. In the first half of the

19th century it was also used for granite from Haytor Quarry. The stone was brought to Teigngrace along a tramway made of granite and then sent on barges down the canal and the River Teign to the docks at Teignmouth.

Cross a couple of boardwalks and enter some trees. You then go through a kissing-gate into a field and pass a path junction; go straight on. A little more than ½ mile after joining the canal you will find a **Templer Way** signpost alongside an interpretation board. Turn left here and cross a bridge and a railway line and go through a gate. Bear left

Drive and Stroll

along a gravel drive and at the road at the end turn right. After 200 yards turn left through two gates, following the Templer Way sign. Cross a field to another kissing-gate and turn right along a track into a wood. When you emerge from the wood, you get a good view to the right. You join another track; go right and at the next fork bear right again. The track becomes a path between fields and re-enters the woods at **Stover Country Park**. After ¼ mile you come out at the path around the lake. Turn left and follow the lakeside back to the car park.

Places of Interest Nearby

About ½ mile down the road is **Trago Mills shopping complex**, which also has a family leisure park. Telephone: 01626 821111. The **Devon Guild of Craftsmen's Riverside Mill**, with displays of work, can be found in Bovey Tracey, 2½ miles away. Telephone: 01626 832223.

15 Ditsworthy Warren

Dartmoor ponies at Drizzle Combe

The Walk 2¾ miles   **Terrain** Mainly level tracks
Map OS Explorer OL28 Dartmoor (GR 578673)

How to get there

The walk starts at the parking area a mile to the east of the village of Sheepstor. Turn south off the B3212 Yelverton to Princetown road at Dousland and follow the signs for Sheepstor. Go through the village, and about ½ mile beyond it, as the road swings right, branch left, following the sign for Nattor. **Parking**: In the parking area at the end of this road.

Drive and Stroll

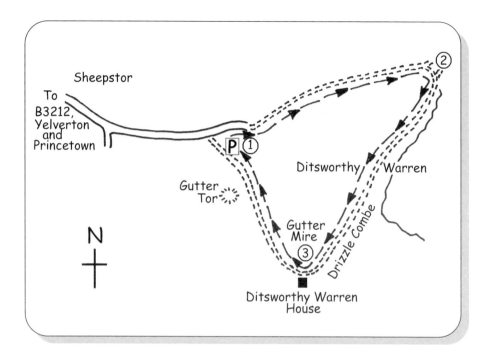

Introduction

This easy route gives you a taste of the best of Dartmoor – extensive views in all directions, wide open spaces, and the opportunity to explore a variety of remains which give you some idea of the lives of the moormen of old. It takes you out along an ancient transmoor route to Ditsworthy Warren and down the delightfully named Drizzle Combe, with signs of prehistoric life visible across the valley. An easy track brings you back past the waste of the equally intriguingly named Gutter Mire and the bulk of Gutter Tor.

The Royal Oak

This ancient hostelry can be found in Meavy, just 2¼ miles west of the start of the walk. It opens straight onto the village green, which is ideal in good weather, as customers can enjoy their drinks out in the sun. Inside there are two rooms: a carpeted lounge and a slate-floored bar. The latter has an enormous fireplace with an inglenook, and the whole pub is decorated with old photographs. The food on offer ranges from soup, jacket potatoes and baguettes to a range of main courses, including fish, lamb and steak. Telephone: 01882 852944.

THE WALK

Go straight on from the parking area, cross a small bridge and continue up the track on the other side. You are now on an ancient transmoor route called the **Jobbers' Road**.

Before the 18th century there were virtually no roads across Dartmoor, only rough tracks. There are a large number of these transmoor tracks still visible, many of which have names relating to their main original purpose. Along the southern edge of the moor ran the Jobbers' Road. Used by wool jobbers, it probably dates from the 13th century. The jobbers collected wool from the farms along the route and took it to Sheepstor, which at that time was an important centre in the wool trade.

Pass a Scout hut on your right and climb gently, with an excellent view to the left, dominated by a range of tors: **Sheeps Tor**, **Down Tor** and **Combshead Tor**. Cross a leat. As you come over the rise you get a superb view to the right to complement the one to the left. This is a typical Dartmoor view: the open moor with not a road, not a house, not a tree in sight, just the rolling hills and the vault of the sky above it.

After ¾ mile you will see a short stone pillar by the side of the track on the left (one of a series erected by the Plymouth City Water Works to mark the extent of the Burrator Reservoir catchment). Turn right here along another track. After a short distance you come to another track; turn right. You pass the remains of a tin-smelting house on the left.

Tin mining was a mainstay of the Dartmoor economy for many centuries. The miners worked the stream beds, panning for the precious ore, and there are few streams or rivers on the moor without their related mining remains. There was a major works at Eylesbarrow Tin Mine, ½ mile to the north-east, and this site was part of that complex, where the ore was smelted to extract the metal.

Continue along the track down the shallow valley of **Drizzle Combe**. There is now a good view ahead, with **Shavercombe Tor** and the two **Trowlesworthy Tors** dominating the scene, and the china clay works of **Lee Moor** on the skyline. On the slopes of the former, half left, you can see the remains of a prehistoric settlement, with its associated field system. Cross a leat, and across Drizzle Combe on your left you will see a stone row and a standing stone.

Over 70 stone rows have been identified on Dartmoor, dating back to around 2500 BC. No one is quite

Drive and Stroll

A kennel in which a warrener would keep his dogs

74

sure what their purpose was, but they appear to have had some ritual significance, perhaps linked to burial – they are very often associated with burial sites. Standing stones are less common, but there are nevertheless a number of them on the moor. As with the rows, no one is quite sure exactly what their role was in the lives and beliefs of the people of that time, but that they had some religious significance is almost certain.

Soon your track merges with another, and you come out at **Ditsworthy Warren House**.

Continue past the house, noticing the openings in the wall of the enclosure on the left; these were the kennels in which the warrener kept his dogs. Just beyond the house you join a much clearer track, alongside which you will see a series of mounds. These are called buries.

The buries were constructed of rock, earth and turf to encourage the rabbits to burrow in a place that was accessible to the warrener. The rabbits were 'harvested' in winter. The warrener would place nets over the buries' entrance holes while the rabbits were out feeding, and then let his dogs loose. They would chase the rabbits, which headed for home and were caught in the nets.

The track curves right and crosses **Gutter Mire**. It skirts the slopes of **Gutter Tor**, and soon you will see the parking area half right. You can cut across to it when there is a gap in the bracken and gorse, or continue along the track to the road and turn right to reach it.

Place of Interest Nearby

About 6 miles to the west of the walk's start is the National Trust property of **Buckland Abbey**, once Sir Francis Drake's home. Telephone: 01822 853607.

16 Bere Alston and the River Tamar

The River Tamar and Cotehele Quay

The Walk 4 miles   **Terrain** Mainly level lanes and clear paths
Map OS Explorer 108 Lower Tamar Valley (GR 446668)

How to get there

Turn west off the A386 between Plymouth and Yelverton and follow the signs to Bere Alston, or turn south onto the B3257 from the A390 Tavistock to Callington road at Gulworthy. **Parking**: In the free car park by the parish hall in Station Road.

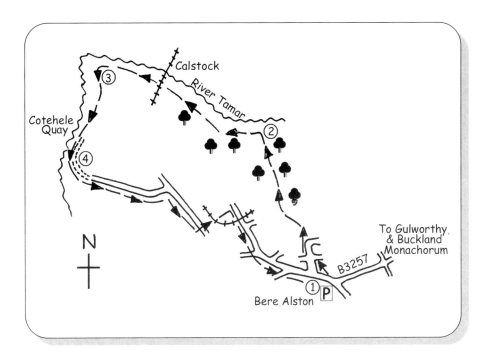

Introduction

This is a lovely hidden corner of Devon, right against the Cornish border and alongside the River Tamar. This varied walk takes you across farm fields to a pretty wood and down to the river. You follow more woodland paths above the water and then wander along the riverbank itself, with the National Trust's Cotehele estate on the opposite side. A view of the attractive Cotehele Quay is followed by another woodland stretch, before tracks, lanes and paths return you to Bere Alston. The going is relatively easy, and there are some lovely views along the way.

The Drake Manor Inn

Although there is a pub in Bere Alston, it does not serve food. However, in Buckland Monachorum, about 3 miles away, you will find the Drake Manor Inn. It is an attractive, low-beamed 16th century hostelry comprising a row of small rooms: a public bar with games and a wood-burning stove; a carpeted snug lounge also with a wood-burning stove, and with an interesting array of miniature cups hanging from the beams; and a slate-floored dining room furnished with pine tables and chairs. Outside is a beer garden. The menu is wide-ranging: from bar snacks such as baguettes and ploughman's lunches to steaks, fish dishes and home-made steak and kidney pie. They have an extensive collection of whiskies and a wide range of wines. Telephone: 01822 853892.

THE WALK

Turn left from the car park, and then after a short distance take the next turning on the right. At the top you come to Broad Park Road; go straight across to a lane, marked as unsuitable for wide vehicles. After 100 yards, as the lane turns sharp right, go left through a gate marked with an apple waymark. Follow the path down between fences, with a superb view up ahead to the majestic **Calstock Viaduct** across the River Tamar. At the end, follow the hedge-lined path which leads into a wood and swings left to a track. Go straight on and at the fork after a few yards bear right, following the yellow public footpath waymark. At the next fork bear left, still following the yellow waymark. When the track ends at a gate, go right down a narrower path into a pretty wood. You descend between banks, go through a barrier and continue to descend on the other side. Go through a gate at the end and to the right of some cottages, and then to the left in front of them.

You now have the **River Tamar** on your right, and just past the cottages you enter another wood.

After 200 yards the path swings to the left to cross a stream and you come to a track; cross over and continue alongside the river. You can see the viaduct between the trees. The path now runs high above the river and then descends. Join a track and leave the wood. Soon you pass a house. When you reach the barn beyond it, turn right through a gate and keep to the right of a field. When you reach the river, turn left along a permissive path which runs along the bank. You now have the river on your right, with **Calstock** on the opposite bank. After ½ mile the river swings left and the path follows it.

On the opposite bank now are the woods of the **Cotehele** estate.

This estate, now owned by the National Trust, was once home to the Edgcumbe family, and contains many interesting old buildings, some dating from the 15th century. Most of them are not visible from the river, but hidden among the trees you can just see an old chapel.

After a while you will find that you cannot continue along the bank any longer, and you will see a stile on the left with a black waymark; cross it into a field and turn right. At the end of the field go through a gate and continue along the right-hand side of the next field. At the end, cross a stile into a wood. You now have **Cotehele Quay** across the river.

The River Tamar seen from the walk

The quay, which used to serve the estate, is an attractive collection of old buildings. Moored alongside is the restored Tamar barge Shamrock.

Follow a track through the wood for about 200 yards, and when it forks go left to leave the river. Soon you emerge from the wood through a gate. Follow another track in front of a house, through another gate and onto a lane. There is now a good view down the river. The lane takes you past a farm to a T-junction; turn right. After ¼ mile you will see a public footpath sign pointing left. Follow it through a kissing-gate and keep to the left of a field. At the end bear left to go under a railway line and through another kissing-gate. Bear right beyond it and cut across a field. Cross a stile at the end into a lane and turn right. Go under the railway line and at the junction by the station go straight on. At the next junction follow the main road round to the left and into **Bere Alston**. Follow this road for another 500 yards, and you will find the car park on your left.

Places of Interest Nearby

About 3 miles away is the National Trust property of **Buckland Abbey**, once the home of Sir Francis Drake. Telephone: 01822 853607. Just beyond is the **Garden House**, a beautiful themed garden. Telephone: 01822 854769.

17 The River Wash and Bow Creek

Bow Bridge

The Walk 2¾ miles   **Terrain** A steady climb at the start, but otherwise relatively level
Map OS Explorer OL20 South Devon (GR 812565)

How to get there

The walk starts at Bow Bridge. Turn south off the A381 Totnes to Kingsbridge road just outside Totnes and follow the signs for Bow Bridge. **Parking**: Customers may leave their cars in the Waterman's Arms car park (but please ask first). For non-customers, there is limited parking in the lane on the other side of Bow Bridge from the pub.

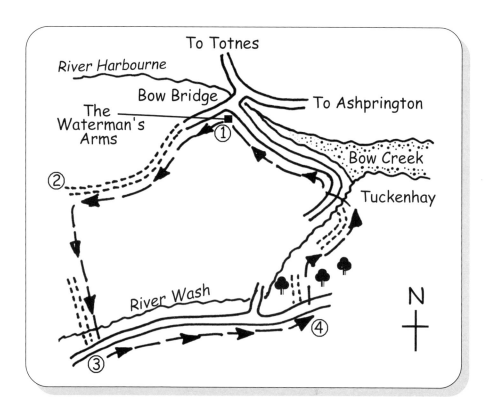

Introduction

This delightful country ramble starts at a picturesque riverside pub at the head of Bow Creek and takes you up fairly steeply onto the hillside above, where there is a superb view across the rolling South Hams farmland. You then descend to the little River Wash, a tributary of Bow Creek, and follow a lane alongside it. After a cool woodland stretch you come out at the pretty hamlet of Tuckenhay and follow the lane alongside Bow Creek, with a chance to enjoy its bird life, to return to Bow Bridge.

The Waterman's Arms

This is a delightful, and surprisingly spacious, old inn, just across the road from the river. It was once feared and avoided as the favourite haunt of naval press gangs, but today there is a very much warmer welcome. The indoor accommodation is full of character. It comprises a fascinating series of interconnected rooms: two quarry-tiled bars, one with a fire, and two carpeted lounges. Low beams are a feature throughout, and the walls are decorated with prints. Across the road there is a riverside terrace, and alongside the pub a beautiful garden. There is a range of bar snacks, including paninis, wraps and baguettes, and a full restaurant menu in the evenings. Telephone: 01803 732214.

THE WALK

Turn left as you leave the pub and immediately left again up a lane marked 'No through road for motor vehicles'. The lane climbs steadily out of the valley. You pass some houses and a farm and the lane finally ends at a gate and becomes an unsurfaced track. Towards the top, as the track swings sharply to the right, look out for a public footpath sign on the left.

Turn off here, go through a gate and keep to the left of the field beyond, along a track. You now get a very pretty view across the countryside ahead of you. Follow the hedge on the left round to the left and go through a gate. Keep to the left again, descending all the time, and go through two gates. The track now runs between a hedge on the left and a fence on the right to another two gates and into a farmyard. Go through that to join a tarred track, which soon takes you out onto a lane. Turn left.

There is a constant variety of wild flowers in the hedgerow as you follow this lane. After ½ mile you come to a junction; go straight on (signposted to Cornworthy and Dittisham). Follow the lane round to the left and then to the right. When you come to the entrance to a house called **Edgecombe Barn** on the left turn off and pass the house down a green lane alongside it.

The green lane runs between high banks and takes you into a pretty little wood. It descends through the trees and emerges onto a track; bear right. The track joins a lane and you pass the old **paper mills** on your left.

These buildings were erected in the early 19th century as woollen mills, but were converted to paper mills in 1829. The clock tower dates from 1889. The mills were closed in 1970 and are now holiday cottages.

When the main lane swings left to join a road, bear right along a smaller lane. Just before the garage at the end, bear right up into another small wood. After a short distance you will come to a junction; turn left down another track. This takes you to a road, which in turn crosses a stream and comes out at a T-junction. Turn right and follow the lane through the delightful hamlet of **Tuckenhay**. The lane curves left and runs parallel to **Bow Creek**. Pass the **Maltster's Arms** on the right and then the **Perchwood lime kilns** on the left.

The old paper mill at Tuckenhay

Limestone and culm (low-grade coal) were burnt together in these kilns to produce quicklime, which had a number of uses. As well as being a major component of mortar, it waterproofed cob walls; it was used on farmland to neutralise acid soil and as a disinfectant, and also in the manufacture of paper. The kilns often acted as a social centre because in winter villagers gathered around them for warmth.

A few hundred yards beyond the lime kilns, you will find the **Waterman's Arms** on the left.

Places of Interest Nearby

About a mile away towards Totnes is **Bowden House**, which combines a photographic museum with ghostly tales and exhibitions. Telephone: 01803 863664. In Totnes itself, 2½ miles away, is **Totnes Castle**, an English Heritage property. Telephone: 01803 864406. Just beyond Totnes is **Dartington Hall**, with its beautiful gardens, which are open to the public all year round. And about 4 miles in the other direction, towards Dartmouth, you will find **Woodlands Leisure Park**. Telephone: 01803 712598.

18 Heybrook and Wembury Bays

Plymouth Sound

The Walk 3¾ miles   **Terrain** A steady climb in the middle
Map OS Explorer OL20 South Devon or OS Explorer 108 Lower Tamar Valley (GR 491498)

How to get there

Turn south-west off the A379 Plymouth to Kingsbridge road at Elburton, following the signs to Staddiscombe and then to Down Thomas. Just past the Down Thomas village sign turn right down Bovisand Lane, following the sign for Bovisand. At the end of that lane turn left into the Bovisand Park holiday complex (you will have to pay a parking fee to get in). **Parking**: Go right through the complex and park at the far end.

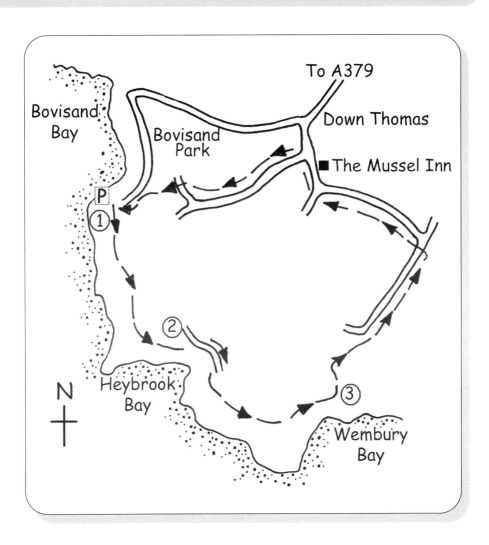

Introduction

The views on this walk start as soon as you step out of your car, and will continue to surprise and dazzle you for much of the route. On the outward journey you can look out to your right across Plymouth Sound to Cornwall, as well as up it to the city. As you round Heybrook Bay and Wembury Point the outlook changes and Wembury Bay and the Yealm estuary come into sight. After a climb inland to Down Thomas the view is across farm fields before you descend back to the coast and the panorama across the sound again.

Drive and Stroll

And to add to the interest, the whole coastal stretch is within the Wembury Marine Conservation Area.

The Mussel Inn

You pass this 14th century hostelry as you walk through Down Thomas. It is a long building divided into three sections. In the middle, as you enter, is a slate-floored bar with comfortable seats and an open fire, and at each end are carpeted dining areas. The main one, to the left, is raised and warmed by a wood-burning stove. There are tables outside, and further down, beyond the car park, a lovely lawned garden with a children's play area. The menu is imaginative, and ranges from baguettes and jacket potatoes with a variety of interesting fillings to fish, meat and vegetarian main courses. In view of the pub's name, it is hardly surprising that their speciality is mussels, but they also serve a range of other fish, straight from the boats, and meat from local farms. Telephone: 01752 862238.

THE WALK

Leave the car park at the far end, following the Coast Path sign.

From here you can see across Plymouth Sound and up to the city. Note the 19th century defences: on the Cornish side of the sound is Picklecombe Fort; much closer, across Bovisand Bay, is Bovisand Fort; and in the middle of the sound is Plymouth Breakwater. These forts were part of a string of fortifications which also stretched around the northern edge of the city. The high walls on the hill above Bovisand Fort were the butts of a firing range.

After about ¼ mile you come to a path junction; go straight on round the headland. At the next junction go straight on again, and about ¾ mile after setting out you will come to an unsurfaced track at **Heybrook Bay**. Follow it to its junction with a surfaced lane. Turn right along **Marine Drive**, following the Coast Path sign.

Follow Marine Drive round to the right; at the path junction, go straight on. At the end of the road bear right, following the Coast Path sign. On your left as you go round the headland is the **HMS *Cambridge*** naval station, and on your right the rocks and shore of the **Wembury Marine Conservation Area**.

This area comprises 4 miles of seashore and the coastal waters along it. Its wide range of habitats support a diversity of plant and animal species, including the

The Mussel Inn, Down Thomas

bloody-eyed velvet swimming crab, the blenny (a fish that lives out of water) and the bladder wrack seaweed.

Soon a new view opens up ahead, across **Wembury Bay** to **Wembury** village and along the coast to the estuary of the River Yealm.

About ¾ mile after leaving Heybrook Bay you will come to a path junction; turn left to leave the coast (signposted to Spring Road). About 200 yards further on, at the next path junction, turn right, following the sign for path number 30. You climb fairly steeply up a pretty green lane. It emerges onto a lane; turn right. After 700 yards turn left down another lane (signposted to Gabber). After another 700 yards you come to **Down Thomas**. At the T-junction turn right (signposted to Staddiscombe and Plymstock). After a couple of hundred yards you will come to the **Mussel Inn** on the right. Just beyond the pub you will find **Manor Bourne Road** on the left; turn down it. You now get good views across farm fields and soon you will

Drive and Stroll

The Great Mew stone

see the sea ahead of you. When you reach the gate for Manor Bourne turn right along another lane, following the public footpath sign for the beach. When the lane goes right to Andurn, turn left, following the sign for the beach again. You now follow a hedge-fringed path to a barrier, beyond which is a surfaced path and some steps. Go down between houses to the road and turn left to return to the car park.

Places of Interest Nearby

Five miles away is Plymouth with a whole host of attractions, including the **National Marine Aquarium** (telephone: 01752 220084) the **Plymouth Dome** (telephone: 01752 603300) and the historic **Barbican** and **Hoe**.

19 | **Modbury**

Modbury nestles in a valley

The Walk 2½ miles **Terrain** Just a few, relatively easy, climbs
Map OS Explorer OL20 South Devon (GR 657515)

How to get there

Modbury is on the A379 between Kingsbridge and Plymouth. **Parking**:
There are two pay-and-display car parks, one short-stay and one long-
stay, in Poundwell Street, which runs south off the main street through
the town.

Drive and Stroll

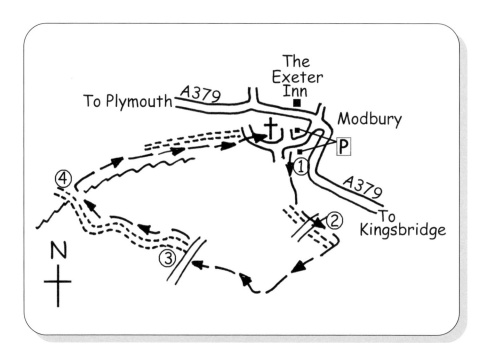

Introduction

One of the many attractive features of the South Hams is the plethora of green lanes that criss-cross the area, which provide havens for wildlife and a wealth of flora. This lovely walk follows a couple of them in the Modbury area, linked by farm paths. In addition to the delights of the hedgerows, there are also several superb views from the higher ground. The going is easy, but there are one or two short hills to negotiate in order to enjoy the views.

The Exeter Inn

This welcoming 14th century coaching inn fronts Church Street, the main street of Modbury. It has three interlinked rooms, all with low ceilings and black beams, and all furnished with tables and padded settles. One of the front rooms boasts a magnificent old fireplace. There is also a very pretty garden to the rear. The food is all home made and ranges from salads, baguettes and jacket potatoes to traditional favourites such as steak and kidney pie, sausage and mash and quiche, as well as a good variety of vegetarian dishes. Telephone: 01548 830239.

THE WALK

The walk starts in the long-stay car park in Poundwell Street. If you have parked in the short-stay car park, turn right and make your way down to it.

Modbury is a pretty town, mainly Georgian in architecture, and was once a centre of the wool trade. It has an interesting 14th century church. Several battles were fought in and around the town during the Civil War.

Go to the far left-hand end of the long-stay car park, where you will find a public footpath sign and a kissing-gate. Go through and follow the path on the other side, alongside a small stream. Go through another gate and across a footbridge, and follow the path round to the left of a house. At the path junction at the end of the wooden fence, go straight on across a stone stile into a field. Cross a leat and aim for a point about halfway along the right-hand boundary. Cross a stile into a sunken lane and turn left.

After a few yards, at the T-junction, go straight across and up a green lane. Climb to a stile, and on the other side turn right and follow the top of a field. You now get a superb view across **Modbury** to **Dartmoor** in the distance. After 100 yards or so, you will see a stile on your left. Cross it and another one, and bear right across a field. As you go over the rise of the field, you will see the stile you should be aiming for on your right. Cross that and another one, and bear left. At the end of the field, bear right through a gate and keep left in the next field. Go through a gate at the end and turn right. About halfway along the hedge you will see a yellow waymark pointing left up the field. As you go you get another magnificent view over to the right, and when you reach the top, a stunning panorama opens up through 180 degrees, with Dartmoor half right and the rolling fields of the **South Hams** to the right. In the far corner is a gate; go through and bear left along the edge of another field. Go through another gate at the end and bear right, downhill. Cross a stile and go down some steps to a lane; turn right.

After a few yards, just beyond the entrance to a farm called **Butland**, go left along a broad track between high hedges. When the track goes right through a gate, go straight on along a narrow green lane. You climb slightly and then begin to descend, winding down into a valley. The green lane broadens to a track and goes down to a lane. Go through a gate and straight on between some buildings (do not turn right along the public bridleway).

Drive and Stroll

 ④

Just beyond the buildings cross the **Ayleston Brook** and turn right, following the public footpath sign. Keep to the right of a field, alongside the brook. When you get to the end, make your way up to a gate towards the top of the hedge. Go through that and another one. Keep to the top of the next field, and at the end you will see a stile on your left. Cross it into a green lane and turn right.

Looking across Modbury to Dartmoor

This green lane is Runaway Lane, so called because during the Civil War, in February 1643, 2,000 Royalist troops escaped down it after a twelve-hour battle with Parliamentary forces in one of the battles of Modbury. It was an incident that led directly to the raising of the siege of Plymouth.

Follow **Runaway Lane** and cross a footbridge. Just beyond it you have a choice: you can either go right up some steps and continue along the top of a field or continue along Runaway Lane. Both routes end at the same point. At the end of the lane or path, turn right along a lane. Pass the church on the left and at the T-junction just beyond turn left. At the next junction, follow the main lane round to the right and at the next go left for the short-stay car park, right for the long-stay one.

Place of Interest Nearby

About 6 miles to the east of Modbury, near Kingsbridge, is the **Sorley Tunnel Adventure Farm**, with a variety of attractions for young children. Telephone: 01548 854078.

20 | East Prawle and Lannacombe Bay

Treacherous rocks near Lannacombe Bay

The Walk 2¾ miles   **Terrain** One steady climb and a rough path along the coast
Map OS Explorer OL20 South Devon (GR 781363)

How to get there

Turn south off the A379 Kingsbridge to Dartmouth road at Frogmore if approaching from Kingsbridge, Stokenham if approaching from Dartmouth, and follow the signs for East Prawle. **Parking**: In the parking area alongside the village green.

Drive and Stroll

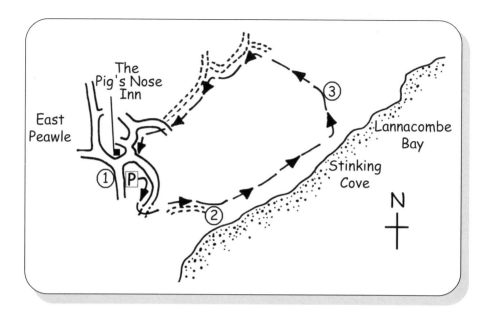

Introduction

This is a short but delightful stroll along this interesting and rugged coastline – renowned for its wrecks. Green lanes and paths take you down to the South West Coast Path, from where you get lovely views along the coast. Passing below steep, rocky slopes, you reach Long Cove, where you turn inland. More pretty paths, green lanes and tracks bring you back to East Prawle.

The Pig's Nose Inn

This delightful pub takes its interesting name from a nearby rock – it was changed from the more prosaic Union Hotel in the 1930s. It has the low ceilings and blackened beams one would expect in a hostelry that is some 500 years old. With stone walls and a flagstoned floor, the main bar oozes atmosphere. There are knick-knacks everywhere, a wood-burning stove, and comfortable tables and magazines to make your stay more enjoyable. Towards the back is a family room with a box of toys for children, and to the side a pool room. Tables outside, overlooking the village green, complete the accommodation. The food is all freshly made, and the menu changes daily. The fare ranges from ploughman's lunches and soup to fresh fish and the Italian main courses that are a speciality. Telephone: 01548 511209.